Words for Life

Words for Life

CONNIE HARRISON

ELEMENT

Shaftesbury, Dorset ● Rockport, Massachusetts

© Connie Harrison 1992

Published in Great Britain in 1992 by
Element Books Limited
Longmead, Shaftesbury, Dorset

Published in the USA in 1992 by
Element, Inc
42 Broadway, Rockport, MA 01966

Cover painting 'Woman with a Yellow Jacket'
by August Macke 1887–1914
Courtesy of Museum Der Stadt, Ulm
Cover design by Max Fairbrother
Calligraphy by Connie Harrison
Printed and bound by
Billings Ltd, Hylton Road, Worcester

British Library Cataloguing in Publication Data

Harrison, Connie
Words for life.
I. Title
398.921

Library of Congress Catalog Card Number available

ISBN 1–85230–312–3

To Carol,
whose loyalty and love,
have given comfort
and support.

I would like to thank
my parents for a
happy childhood,
and my husband
for love and support
during our married years.
Special thanks to teachers
past and present
for knowledge and wisdom
given so generously.
Thank you also to my daughter
Carol, Molly Hanford,
Ethel Ellins and Mary Sutton
and many friends who have
supported and helped.

Introduction

The bird
must break its shell
before it can fly,
and butterflies must struggle
from the chrysalis.
Seeds must burst through
their case
to grow and flower.

In the words of
Kahlil Gibran
"And when the earth
shall claim your limbs
then shall you truly
dance."

Lead me from the unreal
to the real.
Lead me from darkness
to light.
Lead me from death
to immortality.

THE UPANISHADS

Life
is merely a bridge.
Do not
build a house upon it.

CHINESE SAYING

Comfort yourself
with the thought
that suffering
lays bare
the real nature of things,
that it is the price
to be paid
for a deeper more truthful
insight into life.

EUGENIA GINZBURG

What is life?
It is the flash
of a firefly in the night.
It is the breath of a buffalo
in the wintertime.
It is the little shadow
which runs across the grass
and loses itself
in the sunset.

CROWFOOT

Die consciously
before you die.
Put your life
into a chalice
and pour it out
to the world.

RESHAD FEILD

Too much sunshine
makes a desert.
In sorrow
we discover the things
which really matter;
In sorrow
we discover
ourselves.

ARAB PROVERB

Peace
Serenity
Tranquillity
is within you
Look not without for it.

Now is the time to find it
Not tomorrow
Or when everything
is flowing smoothly.

EILEEN CADDY

That thou mayest have
pleasure in everything,
seek pleasure in nothing.
That thou mayest know
everything
seek to know nothing
That thou mayest possess
all things,
seek to possess nothing.
That thou mayest
be everything,
Seek to be nothing.

ST JOHN OF THE CROSS

When we forgive someone,
the knots are untied
and the past is released.

RESHAD FEILD

The owl
whose night – bound eyes
are blind unto the day
cannot unveil
the mystery of light.
If you would indeed
behold the spirit of death,
open your heart wide
unto the body of life.
For life and death are one,
even as the river
and the sea
are one.

KAHLIL GIBRAN

I have desired to go
Where springs not fail,
To fields
where flies no sharp
and sided hail
And a few lilies blow.

And I have asked to be
Where no storms come,
Where the green swell
is in the havens dumb,
And out of the swing
of the sea.

GERARD MANLEY HOPKINS

When you are joyous,
look deep into your heart
and you will find
it is only that
which has given you sorrow
that is giving you joy.
When you are sorrowful
look again in your heart
and you shall see
that in truth
you are weeping
for that which has been
your delight.
Some of you say
"Joy is greater than sorrow,"
and others say,
"Nay, sorrow is the greater."

But I say unto you
they are inseparable.
Together they come,
and when one sits alone
with you at your board,
remember
that the other is asleep
upon your bed.
Verily you are suspended
like scales
between your sorrow
and your joy.
Only when you are empty
are you
at a standstill
and balanced.

KAHLIL GIBRAN

When thou passest
through the waters,
I will be with thee;
and through the rivers,
they shall not overflow thee:
when thou walkest
through the fire,
thou shalt not be burned;
neither shall the flame
kindle upon thee.

AUTHORISED VERSION BIBLE
Isaiah 43.2

But pleasures
are like poppies spread—
You seize the flow'r,
its bloom is shed;
Or like the snow falls
in the river—
A moment white—
then melts forever.

ROBERT BURNS

Nothing can bring you peace
but yourself.

RALPH WALDO EMERSON

All forms that perish
other forms supply,
By turns we catch
the vital breath, and die
Like bubbles on the sea
of Matter born,
They rise, they break,
and to that sea return.

ALEXANDER POPE

The truest end of Life,
is, to know the Life
that never ends.

WILLIAM PENN

The truest view
of life
has always seemed
to me
to be that
which shows that
we are here not to enjoy,
but to learn.

F W ROBERTSON

Walk in the light
and thou shalt see
thy path,
though thorny, bright;
for God, by grace,
shall
dwell in thee,
and
God himself
is light.

B BARTON

When outer symbols
Of communication fail,
Why not try
silence?

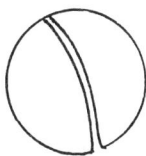

CATHERINE HEWITT

Now
is the only time there is.
No longer
dwell on the past
Nor look
for some future good.

EILEEN CADDY

When we have the courage
to realize that life itself is
the teacher
the timeless Truth
lying within the moment
can come forth.

RESHAD FEILD

The Little Fish

"Excuse me,"
said an ocean fish.
"You are older than I,
so can you tell me
where to find
this thing
they call the ocean?"
"The ocean,"
said the older fish,
is the thing you are in now."
"Oh, this?
But this is water."

What I'm seeking
is the ocean,"
said the disappointed fish
as he swam away
to search elsewhere.

Stop searching, little fish.
There isn't anything
to look for.
All you have to do is look.

ANTHONY DE MELLO

Life is eternal;
and love is immortal;
and death is only a horizon;
and a horizon is nothing
save the limit of our sight.

ROSSITER WORTHINGTON RAYMOND

The Lord is in me,
the Lord is in you,
as life is in every seed.

KABIR

Knowledge
by suffering entereth,
And life
is perfected by death.

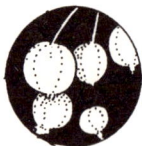

ELIZABETH BARRETT BROWNING

It is eternity now.
I am in the midst of it.
It is about me
in the sunshine;
I am in it,
as the butterfly floats
in the light-laden air.
Nothing has to come;
it is now.
Now is eternity;
now is the immortal life.

RICHARD JEFFERIES

Does the road wind uphill
all the way?
Yes, to the very end.
Will the day's journey
take the whole long day?
From morn to night,
my friend.

But is there for the night
a resting-place?
A roof for when the slow
dark hours begin.
May not the darkness hide it
from my face?
You cannot miss that inn.

Shall I meet other wayfarers
at night?
Those who have gone before.
Then must I knock,
or call when just in sight?
They will not keep you
standing at that door.

Shall I find comfort,
travel-sore and weary?
Of labour
you shall find the sum.
Will there be beds for me
and all who seek?
Yea, beds for all who come.

CHRISTINA ROSSETTI

Flow with the rhythm
of nature
Blend with all there
is around you.

EILEEN CADDY

Other Seas

A fish said to another fish,
"Above this sea of ours
there is another sea,
with creatures
swimming in it-
and they live there
even as we live here"
The fish replied
"Pure fancy! Pure fancy!
When you know
that everything
that leaves our sea
by even an inch,
and stays out of it, dies.
What proof have you
of other lives in other seas?"

KAHLIL GIBRAN

The burden of self
is lightened
when I laugh
at myself.

RABINDRANATH TAGORE

Sorrows
are our best educators.
A man can see further
through a tear
than a telescope.
Grief
should be the instructor
of the wise:
sorrow is knowledge;
they who know the most
must mourn the deepest
o'er the fatal truth,—
the tree of knowledge
is not that of life.

LORD BYRON

Leisure

What is this life if,
full of care,
We have no time
to stand and stare.

No time to stand
beneath the boughs
And stare as long
as sheep or cows.

No time to see,
when woods we pass,
Where squirrels
hide their nuts in grass.

No time to see,
in broad daylight,

Streams full of stars,
 like skies at night.

No time to turn
 at Beauty's glance,
And watch her feet,
how they can dance.

No time to wait
till her mouth can
Enrich that smile
 her eyes began.

A poor life this if,
 full of care,
We have no time
to stand and stare.

WILLIAM HENRY DAVIES

Our chief want in life
is somebody
who shall make us do
what we can.

RALPH WALDO EMERSON

The shell must break
before the bird can fly.

ALFRED LORD TENNYSON

Life
is like
playing a violin
solo in public
and learning
the instrument
as one goes on.

SAMUEL BUTLER THE YOUNGER

Time
is but the stream
I go a-fishing in.

HENRY DAVID THOREAU

The same stream of life
that runs
through my veins
night and day
runs through the world
and dances
in rhythmic measures.
It is the same life
that shoots in joy
through the dust
of the earth
in numberless blades
of grass
and breaks
into tumultuous waves
of leaves and flowers.

RABINDRANATH TAGORE

Humour is the great thing,
the saving thing after all,
the minute it crops up,
all our hardnesses yield,
all our irritations
and resentments
slip away
and a sunny spirit
takes their place.

MARK TWAIN

God "dances" creation.
He is the dancer,
creation is his dance.
The dance is different
from the dancer;
yet it has no existence
apart from him.
You cannot take it home
in a box
if it pleases you.

The moment the dancer
stops,
the dance ceases to be.

Be silent and contemplate
the dance.

Just look:
a star, a flower,
a fading leaf, a bird, a stone...
any fragment of the dance
will do.
Look.
Listen.
Smell.
Touch.
Taste.
And, hopefully,
it won't be long
before you see
him
-the dancer himself!

ANTHONY DE MELLO

Spring –
an experience
in immortality.

HENRY DAVID THOREAU

The only way
to have a friend
is to be one.

RALPH WALDO EMERSON

The silence
Which vibrates around
Contains more sense
of presence
Than sound.

CATHERINE HEWITT

If we could really penetrate
the truth
about impermanence
our life would be lived
very differently.
We could live with more joy
and spontaneity -
able to rejoice
in the continuously
emerging wonder of life.
We could learn
to flow with life's
ups and downs
because we know them
to be changing situations.

It is not that life changes
but that change
is the very essence of life.

Change
and impermanence
are the fundamental
characteristics of life—
which we need to learn
to be in harmony with
in order to be free and
untroubled. Some people
may be frightened to
investigate or accept change.

Yet the joy
and freedom which come
from realising
the truth of change
far surpass
the mundane happiness
of holding on to
illusions and dreams.
Change is life.
Change is the wonder of life.

AJAHN TIRADHAMMO

I am with you
Whether you ascend
to the heights
Or sink to the depths
I am there.

EILEEN CADDY

Your past is burned
in the fire of the present.

RESHAD FEILD

The voice of Nature
loudly cries,
And many a message
from the skies,
That something in us
never dies.

ROBERT BURNS

Don't be dismayed
at good-byes
A farewell is necessary
before you can
meet again.
And meeting again,
after moments or lifetimes,
is certain
for those who are friends.

RICHARD BACH

Compassion
is being in tune
with oneself,
the other person(s)
and the whole world.
It is goodness at its most
intuitive and unreflective.
It is a harmony which opens
itself and permits
the flowing out of love
towards others
without asking any reward.

DAVID BRANDON

All my possessions
for a moment of time.

LAST WORDS ELIZABETH I,
QUEEN OF ENGLAND

"Night is over,
and we children of night
must die
when dawn comes leaping
upon the hills;
and out of our ashes
a mightier love shall rise.
And it shall laugh
in the sun,
and it shall be deathless."

KAHLIL GIBRAN

Life's a voyage
that's homeward bound.

HERMAN MELVILLE

When to the new eyes
of thee
All things
by immortal power,
Near and far,
Hiddenly
To each other linkèd are,
That Thou canst not
stir a flower
Without troubling
of a star...

FRANCIS THOMPSON

Let go of any feeling
of being tied to time
Flow with it
And you will be
in the right place
At the right time
Doing the right thing.

EILEEN CADDY

Speak to Him thou
for He hears,
and Spirit with Spirit
can meet-
Closer is He
than breathing,
and nearer than hands
and feet.

ALFRED LORD TENNYSON

"Help us to find God."
"No one
can help you there."
"Why not?"
"For the same reason
no one can help
the fish
to find the ocean."

ANTHONY DE MELLO

Swift to its close
ebbs out life's little day;
Earth's joys grow dim,
its glories pass away;
Change and decay
in all around I see;
O Thou who changest not,
abide with me.

HENRY FRANCIS LYTE

The One remains,
the many change and pass;
Heaven's light forever shines,
Earth's shadows fly;
Life, like a dome
of many-coloured glass,
Stains the white radiance
of Eternity.

PERCY BYSSHE SHELLEY

I am the light
of the world:
he that followeth me
shall not walk in darkness,
but shall have
the light of life.

AUTHORISED VERSION BIBLE
John 8.12

Without stirring abroad
One can know
the whole world;
Without looking
out of the window
One can see
the way of heaven.
The further one goes
The less one knows.

LAO TZU

Life is a pure flame,
and we live by
an invisible sun
within us.

SIR THOMAS BROWNE

Look to this day!

Look to this day!
For it is life,
the very life of life.
In its brief course
lie all the varieties
and realities
of your existence:
the bliss of growth,
the glory of action,
the splendour of beauty.

For yesterday
is already a dream
and tomorrow
is only a vision,
but today, well-lived,
makes every yesterday
a dream of happiness,
and every tomorrow
a vision of hope.
Look well, therefore,
to this day!
Such is the salutation
of the dawn.

FROM SANSKRIT. AUTHOR AND TRANSLATOR UNKNOWN.

A measure of faith
is whether you can
look at life's darkness
and yet believe in the light.

ANON

There is a Chinese story
of an old farmer
who had an old horse
for tilling his fields.
One day the horse escaped
into the hills
and when
all the farmer's neighbours
sympathized
with the old man
over his bad luck,
the farmer replied,
'Bad luck? Good luck?
Who knows?'
A week later
the horse returned

with a herd of wild horses
from the hills
and this time the neighbours
congratulated the farmer
on his good luck.
His reply was,
'Good luck? Bad luck?
Who knows?'
Then, when the farmer's son
was attempting to tame
one of the wild horses,
he fell off its back
and broke his leg.
Everyone thought this
very bad luck.
Not the farmer,
whose only reaction was,

Bad luck? Good luck?
Who knows?
Some weeks later the army
marched into the village
and conscripted
every able-bodied youth
they found there.
When they saw
the farmer's son
with his broken leg
they let him off.
Now was that good luck?
Bad luck?
Who knows?

ANTHONY DE MELLO

What shall be my legacy?
The blossoms of Spring,
The cuckoo in the hills,
The leaves of Autumn.

MASTER RYOKAN

Ships are safe in harbour,
but that is not
what ships are built for
-to rest calmly
in a harbour.
They only get
barnacle-crusted that way.
They are made to launch out
into the deep.

ANON. FROM 'ALONE' BY KATIE WIEBE.

When the heart weeps
for what it has lost,
the spirit laughs
for what it has found.

ANONYMOUS SUFI APHORISM

Life's play is swift,
Life's playthings fall behind
one by one
and are forgotten.

RABINDRANATH TAGORE

Who can steal the moon!

The Zen master Ryokan
lived a very simple life
in a little hut at the foot
of the mountain.
One night,
when the master
was away,
a thief broke into the hut
only to discover
that there was nothing
to steal
Ryokan returned
and caught the burglar.
"You have put yourself to
much trouble to visit me,"

he said.
"You must not go away
empty-handed.
Please take my clothes and
blanket as a gift."
The thief,
quite bewildered,
took the clothes
and slunk off.
Ryokan sat down naked
and watched the moon.
"Poor fellow,"
he thought to himself,
"I wish I could give him
the gorgeous
moonlight."

ANTHONY DE MELLO

We look before and after,
And pine for what is not;
Our sincerest laughter
With some pain is fraught;
Our sweetest songs
are those
that tell of saddest thought.

PERCY BYSSHE SHELLEY

Life sends up
in blades of grass
its silent hymn
of praise
to the unnamed Light.

RABINDRANATH TAGORE

Place yourself in the middle
of the stream of power
and wisdom
which flows into you as life,
place yourself
in the full centre of that flood,
then you are without effort
impelled to truth,
to right, and a
perfect contentment.

RALPH WALDO EMERSON

Better than a thousand
useless words
is one single word
that gives peace.

Man cannot discover
new oceans
until he has courage
to lose sight
of the shore.

AUTHOR UNKNOWN

Change is taking place
all the time
Do not resist change
But flow with it
Accept it.

EILEEN CADDY

"I am not alone"...
Let this knowledge
inflame you
at every moment.

RESHAD FEILD

Eternity

He who bends
to himself a Joy
Doth the wingèd life
destroy;
But he who kisses
the Joy as it flies
Lives in Eternity's sunrise.

WILLIAM BLAKE

Not till the loom
is silent,
And the shuttles
cease to fly
Shall God unroll
the pattern
And explain
the reason why.

The dark threads
are as needful
In the Weaver's
skilful hand
As the threads
of gold and silver
In the pattern
that He has planned.

AUTHOR UNKNOWN

Nowhere to go
But the next step;
Nothing to do
But take the next breath;
Nothing to be
But what I am;
Nothing to know
But the moment's death.

CATHERINE HEWITT

You can transcend
all negativity
When you realise
that the only power
it has over you
Is your belief in it.
As you experience this truth
about yourself
You are set free.

EILEEN CADDY

To see a World
in a grain of sand,
And a Heaven
in a wild flower,
Hold Infinity
in the palm of your hand,
And Eternity in an hour.

WILLIAM BLAKE

I will not leave you
comfortless:
I will come to you.

AUTHORISED VERSION BIBLE
John 14.18

March the First

Frosty morning–
Robin singing
Blackbird interrupting,
Lorry purring
Train leaving

Peaceful pause–
Hands raised
in adoration
Spirit dancing
All embracing
Held in wonder.

Praise the Lord
For winter passes.
Spring returns,
To melt with fire
The winter of my heart.

ANON

When we rejoice
in our fullness
then we can part
with our fruits
with joy.

RABINDRANATH TAGORE

When we
are in the
present moment,
our work
on Earth
begins.

RESHAD. FEILD

The traveller has reached
the end of the journey!
In the freedom
of the Infinite
he is free
from all sorrows,
the fetters
that bound him
are thrown away,
and the burning fever
of life is no more.

THE DHAMMAPADA

In our eyes,
the dead
are as if they had gone away
for a few years,
or even months.
We apparently lose them,
and this should free
our grasp on the world,
where everything
must eventually be lost.
We shall be beckoned
to the world beyond
where all
shall be found
once more.

ARCHBISHOP FÉNELON
TRANSLATED BY ANTHONY WHITAKER

Needing a teacher?
Turn to your flower garden
See the buds
unfolding naturally.
They do not fret
when cold winds
bow them down.
But gently, and patiently,
await stillness
and the sun's return.
Consider the poppy
So delicate
that you may bend it
to the ground –
Released; up it dances
on its supple stem.

Unperturbed, unharmed,
full of grace and life.
Its small energy determined
on survival.
They flower
in their fullness.
This is the way, this the life.
Be thus open, thus flexible
It is the lifeless,
brittle stick that breaks
with a storm.
It is the rigid, unbending soul
that snaps with adversity.

ANON

You shall see Him
smiling in flowers,
then rising
and waving His hands
in trees.

KAHLIL GIBRAN

O Love
that wilt not
let me go...

GEORGE MATHESON

You are absolutely free
To choose your own path.
Therefore
seek and follow it
And in the end you will
reach the goal:
Your self-realisation
of Me
The divinity
within you.

EILEEN CADDY

All the world's a stage,
And all the men and women,
merely players;
They have their exits
and their entrances,
And one man in his time
plays many parts.

WILLIAM SHAKESPEARE

And
When we stand
On the Shores of Eternity
And look back
Upon our Experiences
In Earthlife,
We will notice
How all the things we did
Happened
In just the right places,
At just the right times:
And
We shall say to Ourselves:
It is Good.

STEPHEN O'BRIEN

Let my doing nothing
when I have nothing to do
become untroubled
in its depth of peace
like the evening
in the seashore
when the water is silent.

RABINDRANATH TAGORE

The mountain
is the mountain
And the Way
is the same
as of old.
Verily what has changed
Is my own heart.

The man who removed
the mountain
began by
carrying away
small stones.

CHINESE PROVERB

Whatsoever things are true,
whatsoever things are honest,
whatsoever things are just,
whatsoever things are pure,
whatsoever things are lovely,
whatsoever things
are of good report;
if there be any virtue,
and if there be any praise,
think on these things.

AUTHORISED VERSION BIBLE
Philippians 4.8

For within you is the light
of the world–
the only light
that can be shed
upon the Path.
If you are unable
to perceive it within you,
it is useless
to look for it elsewhere.
It is beyond you,
because when you reach it
you have lost yourself.
It is unattainable,
because it for ever recedes.
You will enter the light,
but you will never
touch the Flame.

MABEL COLLINS

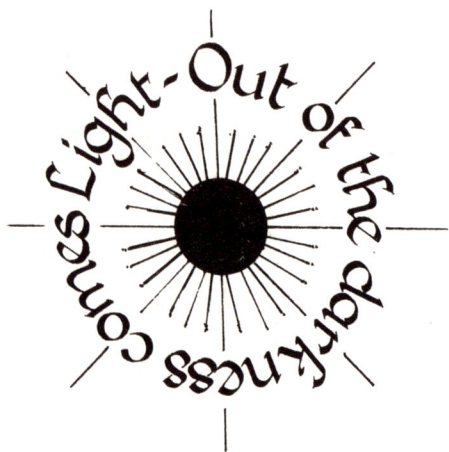

Out of the darkness comes Light

The melody
may change
But
the
D A N C E
goes on...

Peace be unto you.

AUTHORISED VERSION BIBLE
John 20. 19

ACKNOWLEDGEMENTS

The compiler acknowledges with gratitude the courtesy of the following individuals and companies in permitting the use of copyright material.

Bach, Richard, *Illusions: The Adventures of a Reluctant Messiah*, Pan Books Ltd, 1978, by permission of Macmillan Publishers Ltd.

Brandon, David, *Zen in the Art of Helping*, Arkana, Penguin, 1990, by permission of David Brandon.

Caddy, Eileen, *The Living Word*, 1979, reprinted by permission of the Findhorn Press.

Dhammapada, The, translated by Juan Mascaró, Penguin Classics, 1973, © Juan Mascaró, 1973.

Feild, Reshad, *A Travelling People's Feild Guide*, 1986, reprinted by permission of Element Books.

Fénelon, Archbishop, *Letters to Men*, translated by Antony Whitaker, © by permission of Anthony Whitaker.

Ginzburg, Eugenia, *Within the Whirlwind*, reprinted by permission of HarperCollins Publishers.

Hewitt, Catherine, 'We cannot condemn the flame', *Poems by a Lay Buddhist*, by permission of Catherine Hewitt.

Mello, Anthony de, *One Minute Wisdom*, 1985, by kind permission of X. Diaz del Rio S. J., Gujarat Sahitya Prakash, Publishers.

Mello, Anthony de, *The Song of the Bird*, 1984, by kind permission of X. Diaz del Rio S. J., Gujarat Sahitya Prakash, Publishers.

O'Brien, Stephen, *Visions of Another World*, 1989, Aquarian/Thorsons, part of HarperCollins Publishers.

Ryokan, Master, *Zen for Beginners*, (extract from p. 139), Judith Blackston and Zoran Josipovic. Unwin Hyman, part of HarperCollins Publishers.

Tiradhammo, Ajahn, *The Essential Teaching of Buddhism*, ed. Kerry Brown and Joanne O'Brien. By permission of Ajahn Tiradhammo.

Tzu, Lao, *Tao Te Ching*, translated by D. C. Lau, Penguin Classics, 1963. © D. C. Lau, 1963.

Upanishads The, Mentor Books, 1957, Swami Prabhavananda & Frederick Manchester, reprinted by permission of Vedanta Press.

Wiebe, Katie, *Alone. A Search for Joy*, reprinted by permission of Hodder & Stoughton Ltd and Kindred Press.

BIBLIOGRAPHY

Anon. 'A measure of faith', from *Alone*, Katie Wiebe, Hodder & Stoughton Ltd, 1989, and Kindred Press, USA.

Anon. 'A mountain is a mountain.' Traditional Zen training story.

Anon. 'Life is merely a bridge.' Chinese saying.

Anon. 'Look to this day.' Sanskrit.

Anon. 'Man cannot discover new oceans.'

Anon. 'March the First.'

Anon. 'Not till the loom is silent.'

Anon. 'Too much sunshine makes a desert.' Arab proverb.

Anon. 'Ships are safe in harbour' from *Alone* by Katie Wiebe, Hodder & Stoughton Ltd, 1989, and Kindred Press, USA.

Anon. 'When the heart weeps.' Sufi Aphorism.

Anon. 'The man who removed the mountain.' Chinese proverb.

Anon. 'Needing a teacher.'

Bach, Richard, *Illusions: The Adventures of a Reluctant Messiah*, Pan Books Ltd, 1978.

Barton, B., *The New Dictionary of Thoughts*, The Waverley Book Company of London, 1877.

Bible, The Authorised Version.

Blake, William, *The Poetical Works of William Blake*, Oxford University Press, 1913.

Brandon, David, *Zen in the Art of Helping*, Arkana, Penguin, 1990.

Browne, Sir Thomas, *Hydrotaphia, V.*

Browning, Elizabeth Barrett, *A Vision of Poets*, 1844.

Burns, Robert, *Tam O'Shanter The Golden Treasury of Longer Poems*, Everyman's Library, edited by Ernest Rhys, J. M. Dent & Sons Ltd, 1921.

Butler, Samuel, the younger, *Collected Essays*, Vol. II, 1835–1902.

Byron, Lord, *The New Dictionary of Thoughts*, The Waverley Book Company of London, 1877.

Caddy, Eileen, *The Living Word*, The Findhorn Press, 1979.

Collins, Mabel, *Light on the Path*, The Theosophical Publishing House Ltd, 1972.

Crowfoot, Last words (1890).

Davies, William Henry, 'Leisure', *Albatross Book of Verse*, William Collins, 1933.

Dhammapada, The, translated by Juan Mascaró, Penguin Classics, 1973.

Elizabeth 1st, Queen of England, Last words (1603).

Emerson, Ralph Waldo, *Self Reliance – Essays*, Everyman's Library, J. M. Dent & Sons Ltd, 1972.

Emerson, Ralph Waldo, *Considerations by the Way – Essays*, Everyman's Library, J. M. Dent & Sons Ltd, 1972.

Feild, Reshad, *A Travelling People's Feild Guide*, Element Books, 1986.

Fénelon, Archbishop, *Letters to Men*, translated by Antony Whitaker.

Gibran, Kahlil, *The Prophet*, William Heinemann Ltd, 1963.

Gibran, Kahlil, *The Forerunner*, William Heinemann Ltd, 1920.

Ginzburg, Eugenia, *Within the Whirlwind*, HarperCollins Publishers.

Hewitt, Catherine, 'We cannot condemn the flame', *Poems by a Lay Buddhist*, published by Catherine Hewitt.

Hopkins, Gerard Manley, *Poems*, Oxford University Press, 1970.

Jefferies, Richard, *The Story of my Heart*, Penguin Illustrated Classics, 1938.

Kabir, *Poems of Kabir*, translated by Rabindranath Tagore, assisted by Evelyn Underhill, Macmillan, 1915.

Lyte, Henry Francis, 'Abide with me' *Methodist Hymn Book*, 1933.

Matheson, George, 'O love that wilt not let me go', *Methodist Hymn Book*, 1933.

Mello, Anthony de, *One Minute Wisdom*, Gujarat Sahitya Prakash, 1985.

Mello, Anthony de, *The Song of the Bird*, Image Books, 1984.

Melville, Herman, Cournos, (Modern Plutarch).

O'Brien, Stephen, *Visions of Another World*, Aquarian/Thorsons, 1989.

Penn, William, *Some Fruits of Solitude*. Source unknown.

Pope, Alexander, 'An Essay on Man', *The Works of Alexander Pope*, London, 1772.

Raymond, Rossiter Worthington, A commendatory prayer. Source unknown.

Robertson, F. W., *The New Dictionary of Thoughts*, The Waverley Book Company of London, 1877.

Rossetti, Christina, 'Uphill' *The Oxford Book of English Verse 1250–1918*, chosen and edited by Sir Arthur Quiller-Couch, Oxford University Press, 1900.

Ryokan, Master, *Zen for Beginners*, text Judith Blackston and Zoran Josipovic, Unwin Paperbacks, 1986.

Saint John of the Cross, 'That thou mayest have pleasure in everything'. Source unknown.

Shakespeare, William, 'As You Like It', *Shakespeare Comedies*, Everyman's Library, edited by Ernest Rhys, J. M. Dent & Sons Ltd, 1906.

Shelley, Percy Bysshe, 'To a Skylark' st. 18, *The Poetical Works of Percy Bysshe Shelley*, Edited by William Michael Rossetti, E. Moxon, Son, & Co.

Shelley, Percy Bysshe, 'Adonais' st. 52, *The Poetical Works of Percy Bysshe Shelley*, edited by William Michael Rossetti, E. Moxon, Son, & Co.

Tagore, Rabindranath, *Collected Poems & Plays*, Macmillan, 1936.

Tennyson, Alfred Lord, 'The High Pantheism', *The Complete Works of Alfred, Lord Tennyson*, Macmillan, 1894.

Tennyson, Alfred Lord, 'The Ancient Sage', *The Complete Works of Alfred, Lord Tennyson*, Macmillan, 1894.

Thompson, Francis, 'The Mistress of Vision'. Source unknown.

Thoreau, Henry David, from 'Where I lived and what I lived for'. Source unknown.

Tiradhammo, Ajahn, *The Essential Teaching of Buddhism*, ed. Kerry Brown and Joanne O'Brien, 1989.

Twain, Mark. Source unknown.

Tzu, Lao, *Tao Te Ching*, translated by D. C. Lau, Penguin Classics, 1963.

Upanishads, The, selected and translated from the original Sanskrit by Swami Prabhavananda and Frederick Manchester, The Vedanta Press, 1957.